DEATH IN THE FREEZER

How exciting to have a new baby in a family! A brother or a sister to play with, someone to tell secrets to, someone to be a friend for all your life.

But Ellen Shore is not happy when her brother Al is born, because her parents think that a son is more important than a daughter. Ellen has food to eat, of course, and new clothes, and dolls to play with – but nobody is interested in her. So Ellen begins to hate her baby brother.

And when she is an adult, she goes on hating him. She has three young kids, no husband, and very little money. But Al is rich. He is a famous rock star now, with lots of expensive cars, a beautiful big house, and a life of parties and travel. Ellen cleans his house, cooks for his parties, even steals drugs for him from the hospital where she works. And Al gives her nothing.

So Ellen begins to make secret plans for her brother. But Al has some very strange friends, who also have plans for him . . .

OXFORD BOOKWORMS LIBRARY
Crime & Mystery

Death in the Freezer

Stage 2 (700 headwords)

Series Editor: Jennifer Bassett
Founder Editor: Tricia Hedge
Activities Editors: Jennifer Bassett and Alison Baxter

TIM VICARY

Death in the Freezer

OXFORD UNIVERSITY PRESS

OXFORD

UNIVERSITY PRESS

Great Clarendon Street, Oxford OX2 6DP

Oxford University Press is a department of the University of Oxford.
It furthers the University's objective of excellence in research, scholarship,
and education by publishing worldwide in

Oxford New York

Auckland Bangkok Buenos Aires Cape Town Chennai
Dar es Salaam Delhi Hong Kong Istanbul Karachi Kolkata
Kuala Lumpur Madrid Melbourne Mexico City Mumbai
Nairobi São Paulo Shanghai Taipei Tokyo Toronto

OXFORD and OXFORD ENGLISH are registered trade marks of
Oxford University Press in the UK and in certain other countries

ISBN 0 19 422969 6

Typeset by Wyvern Typesetting Ltd, Bristol

Printed in Spain by Unigraf S.L.

Illustrated by: Paul Dickinson

CONTENTS

1
Baby Al

I killed a dead man. That's why I'm in prison.

The dead man was my brother, Al. He was born six years after me, and I always hated him, even when he was a baby. Before he was born, my parents loved me. My father carried me on his back, and took me swimming. My mother bought me lots of dolls, and we played with them together. I have seen the photos. My parents took a lot of photos of me, in my first six years. I still have the photos, in a book.

But then Al was born. I have a photo of him, too, as a baby in the hospital, here in Los Angeles. My mother is holding him, and looking at him with a big smile on her face. My father has his arm round my mother, and he is smiling at baby Al, too. Al is holding his daddy's finger.

And me? Where am I in this picture? I am standing by myself, beside the bed, watching them. There is a strange smile on my face. I *think* I am happy, but I'm not sure. And no one is looking at me.

It was always like that, after Al was born. He was a boy, and that was important to my parents – and very important to my Dad. Most of the photos in the book are of Al. Al eating baby food, Al learning to walk, Al on my Dad's back, Al playing football, Al swimming, Al running,

Al having a big party with his friends.

A hundred photos of Al, and five or ten of me.

Of course, my parents played with me sometimes, took me swimming, bought me clothes. But they weren't *interested* in me. Before Al was born, they spent a lot of time with me. After he was born, they didn't.

Often, I played hospitals with my dolls. I played that the dolls were sick, and I was a nurse. When the dolls had bad stomachs, I gave them medicine to take. Sometimes I pulled their arms and legs off and put tomatoes on them, to look like blood. And sometimes I gave them drugs. That was the best of all. My mother gave me an old syringe, and I put water in it and pushed it into the dolls. Soon the dolls were full of holes.

'That's a good game for a little girl,' my mother said. But she didn't understand. Because in my game, all the dolls were boys, like Al. And they never got better. They were sick for a very long time, and then they died. I put them in a hole in the ground, in the garden.

When I was ten, my mother died. My father was unhappy, and began to drink a lot. Sometimes he came home with strange women, but he didn't marry any of them. I think the women didn't like him, because he drank so much. When he wasn't drunk, he played with Al. So I had more time alone.

I was a good girl at school, and I was beautiful too, so I

I put water in the syringe and pushed it into the dolls.

had a lot of boyfriends. My father hated them. 'You stay away from those boys, Ellen!' he shouted. 'It's not right. I don't want them in my house!'

'Why not, Dad?' I asked. 'You bring your women here, don't you? Why can't I bring my boyfriends?'

3

'Shut up, girl!' he shouted. He was very angry. Sometimes he hit me, and once I had to go to the hospital.

So what did Al do, you ask? Him? Nothing. He just watched, and laughed, and played football with Dad.

Then I met John. He was twenty-two years old, and big and strong like Arnold Schwarzenegger. All the girls thought he was wonderful. One day he asked me to go to a party with him – *me!* I was very excited, so I went home, and put on my best clothes and shortest skirt, to look nice for him. Then I heard John's motorbike and went downstairs. Dad was at the door.

'Where are you going?' he asked.

'Out,' I smiled at him. 'With my new boyfriend.'

'Oh no, you're not!' he said. 'Not in that skirt. You're only eighteen, Ellen. I know what boys want.'

'I don't care,' I said. I pushed past him, but he pulled my arm. I screamed, and he hit my face.

Then John came. He was wonderful! He took Dad's arms, held them by his side, and pushed him slowly back into the house. Dad couldn't do anything! John sat him down in a chair, then walked out and put his arms round me. Right there, in front of the house!

Then we rode away on his motorbike.

Then John came. He was wonderful!

2
Wild Boys

I never went home again. That night I stayed in John's apartment, and three months later I knew that I was going to have his baby. But I lost that baby at five months, and soon I went back to finish my training as a nurse. Four years later, I had another baby, and this one was born all right. Now I'm twenty-nine, and I have three small kids.

But I'm not really happy. John is a good-looking man, a wonderful lover, but . . . I'm not his only woman. I know he has two other girlfriends, and both of them have babies. Maybe there are more. Sometimes I don't see him for weeks, and then he comes back and smiles and tries to be nice to me, but I still get angry. He doesn't have a real job and we have very little money. I work as a nurse in a hospital, but I don't get much for that. And I have to pay half of it to someone to look after my kids while I'm at work.

Dad died four years ago. Al told me about it. 'Dad had a heart attack,' he said. 'He was really angry about John, so he began running to try to get stronger. But he didn't stop drinking. Then one day he drank half a bottle of whisky, went for a run, came home, and fell down dead on the floor!'

Al laughed. How strange, I thought. Dad loved Al, but

when he died, Al laughed. Perhaps men are just animals, really, not people like us.

When Dad was dead, I saw Al more often. I didn't like him much, but he was my only family. Sometimes we went swimming together with the kids, or out for a pizza. John didn't like me to talk to other men, but Al was OK, because he was my brother.

When Al was eighteen, he began a rock band, *Wild Boys*. He sang, and played guitar. At first they played in small restaurants, and then they made a record. Lots of people bought it. The band began to play in front of thousands of people. They made three more records, and travelled all over the world. It was wonderful. By the time he was twenty, my little brother Al was famous, and rich.

He was very, very rich. He bought a yellow Rolls-Royce, a Jaguar, a Porsche, and a house in the best part of Los Angeles with fifteen bedrooms, a tennis court, a swimming pool, and a view over the sea. And he gave me our parents' house.

That was nice, but it wasn't *very* nice. I mean, our parents' house is very old. It has three small bedrooms, a small garden, and is in a noisy, dirty street. It's better than my old apartment, but still . . .

I went to see Al often. He gave me a key, to get in and out of his house. And I cooked for him when he had big parties there. I enjoyed the parties. John came too. There were famous people, wonderful food and music, lots of drink and drugs.

Drugs. Yes, well, the drugs were a bad thing. Al got much too interested in drugs. A lot of his friends took drugs – and my John did, too. And when they were on drugs, they often didn't know what day it was. They did crazy things. I remember one party when they went for a midnight swim down at the beach. The boys took all John's clothes away while he was still in the sea, and drove away with them. So John had to walk back through the streets in the middle of the night, all wet from the sea, while we laughed at him from the car. He was so angry! I thought that was really funny, but John didn't talk to me for a week!

But Al and his friends took more and more drugs, and the music began to get worse. Sometimes Al was still in bed at four o'clock in the afternoon. And when he did get up, he looked very sick. He was thin, his face was white, and he didn't want to eat anything. He asked me to help him.

'You're a nurse, Ellen,' he said. 'I feel sick. Give me some medicine or something! Help me!'

'You don't need medicine,' I said. 'You need a lot of good food, swimming, and *no more drugs!*'

'Who do you think you are, Ellen?' he said. 'My mother or something?'

'No, but I *am* your sister, and a nurse,' I said. 'Listen to

I enjoyed the parties.

me. I'm going to get you some medicine to help you stop
the drugs, and I'm going to cook you a good meal every
day. But you *must* stop the drugs. Try it, Al! It works – I
know it does!'

He did try it, and it helped. After two or three months Al was stronger and happier, and he began to play good music again. He was pleased; he trusted me. Sometimes, in the evenings, he took me and my kids to the beach. We had a meal and drank and went swimming together, and had a good time. Those few months with my brother were a good time in my life.

'Now, at last,' I thought, 'my brother likes me. He's happy and healthy because of me. Maybe he can help me – give me money, buy me a new car and a nice house, take me to Europe with him.'

But of course I was wrong. No one ever gives me anything.

3
The tour

'I'm going away on a tour,' Al said one day. 'All around the USA and Europe, to play music, for four months.'

I looked at him and thought, *he's going to ask me to come too. I can see the world, bring my kids.* 'Wonderful!' I said. 'We can . . .'

'When I'm away, I want you to clean the house for me,' Al said. 'Of course you can't live here, but I want you to come every day to clean. And there's another thing, Ellen.'

'Yes, what?' *So I'm not going, I'm just his cleaner*, I thought. I really hated him then. I wanted to scream – but I didn't. I said nothing.

'You know I get very tired on these tours, and I need drugs to help me play good music. But I don't want to take dangerous drugs, Ellen. I need clean, safe drugs. I want you to get some drugs from the hospital for me. You're a nurse, it's easy for you. Just take them secretly – no one will know.'

'That's a crime, Al,' I said. 'People go to prison for that. Is that what you want me to do? Steal drugs for you, and go to prison maybe?'

'Why not?' He laughed. 'You're my sister, Ellen! And don't forget, I gave you my parents' house, didn't I? What more do you want?'

That's what he said: *my* parents' house, not *our* parents' house! Really, half of it always belonged to me, but Dad gave it all to Al because he was so angry about me and John. But Al didn't think of that. He thought that everything belonged to him, just like when he and I were kids – when he played football with Dad, and I played with my dolls.

I remembered my dolls then, and the syringe with water in it. And I smiled. 'All right, Al, I'll get you something. You're right, you *are* my brother.'

And I looked around, at the beautiful house, and the

When you die, all this is going to belong to me.

swimming pool, and the view of the sea, and I thought: *You're not married, Al, and there's only you and me in our family. So when you die, all this is going to belong to me.*

Al was right. It was easy to steal drugs from the hospital; no one saw me. I also stole syringes, which were all clean and new. Al was very pleased with them.

'Thanks, Ellen,' he said. 'Now I'm going to play lots of good music. I'll be OK now.'

4
The Futures

He went away for four months, and I cleaned his beautiful big house every day. But he didn't phone me once.

And when he came back, he wasn't OK. He looked thin and white and sick. I tried to talk to him, but he didn't listen. I was just the cook and cleaning woman. He had a lot of new friends now. And some of these friends were very strange.

I first met the Futures one night in November. There was a party at Al's house, and when I went there after work, I saw a big black car outside. It looked like a boring car, and when I went inside, I thought the people looked boring too. But that was only on the outside. Inside, they were as dangerous as wild animals.

A businessman in a dark suit sat opposite Al, with a young woman on the arm of a chair beside him. The man was about forty years old with grey hair. The woman was much younger – about twenty-four maybe. She had long black hair, and was wearing a blue dress. At first I thought she was the man's daughter, but then Al said:

'Hi, Ellen! Meet my new friends – Dan Future and his wife Linda. We met in New Mexico.'

There were about ten other people there, talking and listening to music. We had one or two drinks, and Al and Linda went for a swim in the pool. I sat and watched the beautiful evening sun over the sea, and Dan Future sat beside me. We watched Al's thin body when he got slowly out of the pool, and Dan said: 'Life's so very short, don't you think?'

'What do you mean?' I asked.

He smiled; he had beautiful white teeth. 'My father died last year. He was sixty-five. That's not much, is it? Sixty-five years of life.'

'Well, maybe not,' I said. 'But . . .'

'Think how many times the sun has gone down in the evenings. Ten billion times, maybe, a hundred billion? A hundred billion evenings as beautiful as this, but my father sat and watched maybe only a few hundred of them. We only live a short time, like birds, you know.'

'Meet my new friends – Dan Future and his wife Linda.'

'Yes, I see,' I said. I looked at him, surprised. Businessmen don't usually say things like that; but then businessmen didn't usually come to Al's parties. Dan Future's hair was beautifully cut, he had an expensive watch, nice clothes – he looked strong and healthy. Why did he want to talk about death? The only sick person in this house was Al. *What did Dan Future know about that?*

He smiled again. 'We don't have to die, you know. Soon, people are going to live a hundred and fifty years, maybe more. You just need to have money, that's all. I told your brother about it in New Mexico, and he was very interested. Maybe you are, too?'

Oh, no, I thought, *the man's crazy*. 'Are you, er . . . do you belong to one of these new churches?' I asked.

'No, no. I'm a scientist. I can tell you all about it, if you like . . .'

But he didn't, because at that minute Al came up to me, and said: 'We need some more drinks, and food! How about some food, Ellen? There are some hamburgers in the freezer!' And so I went to get them.

Al had the money, and I didn't. And I was a woman. So I got the drinks and cooked, and about ten o'clock I went home. And I didn't learn any more about Dan Future and his crazy ideas. Not then.

But I learned a lot about them, two weeks later.

5
The freezer

It was the night of Al's birthday. I got home about seven.
Then I put the kids to bed, and made supper for John. He
didn't talk to me – he just sat in front of the TV with the
food and his bottles of whisky. So I thought, I'm going
out. I'll go say Happy Birthday to Al. Even Al can't be as
bad as this. And he *is* my brother.

I had some more drugs and syringes for him, from the
hospital, so I put them in nice paper like presents. 'Like
sweets for a baby,' I thought. 'Al's just a big baby, really,
with his music and a lot of expensive cars to play with. Or
a doll. And I'm like his nurse.'

When I got to his house, it was very quiet. There were
only one or two lights on downstairs. And the big black
car was outside.

'That's strange,' I thought. 'It's Al's birthday. Why isn't
there a party?'

I got out of my car and walked to the door. It was open.
There was soft music in the big living room, but no lights
were on. The moonlight came in through the windows,
and I could see the moon in the water in the pool outside.

'Al?' I called. 'Al, where are you?'

No answer. Just the music – quiet, and very beautiful. I
went to Al's room but his bed was empty. All the rooms

17

were empty. I came back to the living room, opened the door to the moonlit garden, and there . . .

Aaaaaaah! I screamed and nearly fell down. Then I stood still and laughed. But nothing happened. I stopped laughing, and it was silent again.

Two people sat on the ground. They sat very still, and held their hands and faces up to the moon. They didn't move, or look at me.

'Al?' I said. 'Al? What are you doing?'

But it wasn't Al, it was a man and a woman. The man's hair was silver in the moonlight, and the woman's hair was long and dark. Dan and Linda Future.

They began to sing. It was a strange song, without words – and they sang for nearly ten minutes. When they finished I said, in a loud voice: 'Where is Al?'

They looked at me then, and got up. Both of them came to me, and took my hands. 'He's asleep,' Dan said. 'We have saved him.'

I took my hands away, afraid. 'What do you mean?' I said. 'What are you talking about?'

'He was very sick,' Dan said. 'He had AIDS. You knew that, didn't you?'

For a minute I couldn't speak. I was afraid. I said: 'No, of course I didn't! When did he get it?'

'Who knows?' Dan said. 'On tour, I think – he took drugs, didn't he? No one can cure AIDS – not yet. But one

18

They held their hands and faces up to the moon.

day, someone's going to find a cure. So we helped him. He is safe now, for hundreds of years! Isn't that good?'

Linda took my hand again. 'Come with me,' she said. 'Let's go and look.'

'But where . . .?'

'Don't be afraid, it's all right.' She smiled; I saw her beautiful white teeth in the moonlight. Then she took me, like a child, into the house, through the living room, and down into the music room.

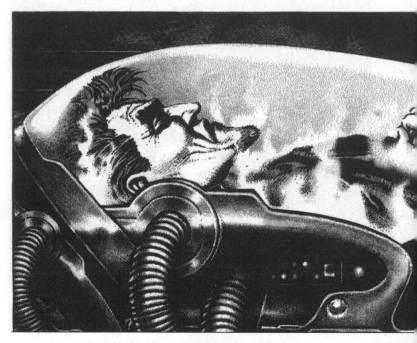

Inside the glass case there was a body.

The music room was in the ground under the house. Al liked to play very loud music all night, so he built the room down there to be quiet. It was a big room with one small window, high up. It was never hot in the summer nor cold in the winter. But now . . .

Now it was different. In the middle of the room there was a big glass case. A cold blue light came from inside it. There was the noise of something large and quiet, like a big freezer. And inside the glass case there was a body.

Al's body. My brother.

The body was lying on a bed of ice inside the case, with its head higher than its feet. It wore silver clothes and its face was blue.

'Oh no! What's happened?' I said.

'It's all right, Ellen,' Linda Future said. 'He isn't dead.'

'Not dead?' I said. 'But . . .'

'He's frozen. He took a sleeping drug, and then we froze him. It is very, very cold in there: −196° Celsius. Nothing happens to bodies as cold as that. Nothing changes for hundreds of years, thousands of years maybe. That's what's going to happen to Al. He's going to stay there for a hundred years, two hundred years maybe. Then one day a doctor can wake him up and cure him. That's what our company does, you know.'

'Your company,' I said. 'What do you mean?'

'I'm sorry, didn't Al tell you?' Dan Future said. He was in the room too now, with his hand on my back. He gave me a business card. It said:

ESCAPE FROM DEATH
The Cryonics Company   *Dan and Linda Future*

'I don't understand,' I said. 'What's cryonics?'

'It's the science of freezing people,' he said. 'That's what we do. We help people like your brother to stay alive for hundreds of years. Then, when the doctors can cure them, they wake up. And we look after their money and houses too.'

'You do *what?*' I said. Suddenly I was very, very angry. *'You look after their money and houses?'*

'Yes.' He smiled, and his beautiful teeth looked blue in the strange light from the freezer. He took a piece of paper out of his pocket. 'It's all here, Ellen. Your brother wrote his name on this paper. It says that we must keep him here, frozen, in this room for two hundred years. By then, there will be a cure for AIDS. For now, we will look after his money and his house, and when we are dead, our company will go on looking after them. Then they will be ready for him when he comes back to life.'

'But . . . you *killed* him!' I screamed. My anger was terrible. 'And now you're stealing his money too – and his house! It belongs to me, not you!'

Dan Future laughed. 'No, no, my dear. You don't understand. The money and the house don't belong to us, or to you. They belong to your brother, Al. He isn't dead, he's just frozen. And he's going to stay frozen for two hundred years.'

He laughed again, and his young wife began to laugh, too. I turned, and walked out of the house.

'The money and the house don't belong to us, or to you.'

6
The Key

Next day, the Futures sent me all the papers with Al's name on. I showed them to John. 'You need a lawyer,' he said. 'These people are criminals.'

So I got a lawyer, but it didn't help. You need money for a good lawyer, and I had nothing. I went to the nearest lawyer's office, but the lawyer was unfriendly and unhelpful. 'It costs $100 for half an hour, and you pay before we talk,' he told me. When I gave him the $100, he took off his watch and put it on the table in front of him.

He was a small man with not much hair and a white, tired face. His eyes were cold and grey, like stones. When I told him my story he said: 'It's not possible.'

'But it's true! Read this!' He read the papers slowly, then smiled and looked at his watch.

'Well, this is very interesting,' he said. 'I agree, these people are criminals. But to get the house, we have to show that your brother is dead.'

'So how can we do that?'

'Well, we can ask scientists to say that cryonics doesn't work. But the Futures are going to have other scientists who say it does work. So we need a doctor to look at your brother's body and say he's dead. That's a better idea.'

I laughed. 'How can a doctor look at the body? It's

'I can't win, because I don't have any money.'

frozen to −196° Celsius. It's just a piece of ice!'

'Yes, well, that is difficult, Ms Shore, I do see that.' The lawyer looked at his watch again. 'It's difficult, but that's what we need to do. But . . .' He looked at the papers again. 'Before we begin, I have to tell you that Dan Future's lawyer is one of the best in the country. Maybe I can win, and maybe I can't. But it's going to cost you a lot of money.'

'How much?' I asked.

'$50,000 – at first. Maybe a lot more later.'

I stood up slowly. 'Forget it,' I said. I only had $300 in the bank, and there was no food in the house. I looked at the lawyer's old, tired face. 'I can't win, can I, because I don't have any money! The Futures are stealing that house from me, and I can't do anything about it!' I ran out of the office.

For a week I was angry – every day, all day. I shouted at people at work, I shouted at the kids. John got drunk, so I dropped a plate of eggs, spaghetti and hamburgers on his head. He hit me, and went to stay with one of his girlfriends. I wasn't sorry – he was stupid and lazy, like all men.

Twice I drove past Al's house, and saw the black car outside. *That house belongs to me!* I thought. *Those people stole it from me! And I can do nothing.*

Nothing?

One night I had a dream. In my dream I saw Al's frozen body, with a key in his mouth. The key was warm, and the ice on Al's frozen head changed to water. Then the key moved, and warmed Al's body too. Al opened his mouth, screamed, and died.

At two o'clock I woke up. It was very quiet. There was moonlight in the room, and no cars were moving on the road outside. I began to think about my dream. *The key!* Of course. Suddenly, I had a plan.

27

*I dropped a plate of eggs, spaghetti and hamburgers
on John's head.*

I got up, put on a black shirt and jeans, and drove to
Al's house. The big black car was outside, but there were
no lights on in the house. I left my car two hundred yards
away, and walked quietly to the door.

The Futures didn't know that I had a key. I opened the
door very quietly, and went into the big living room. There
was no sound – everyone was asleep. My key opened the
music room too – it opened all the doors in the house.

28

I went in, and looked at Al.

He was still there – the silver body and icy blue face in the glass case. The room was full of blue light and the quiet noise of electricity.

Electricity – that was the thing! Al needed electricity in here for his music, and of course the freezer needed a lot of electricity too. Beside the freezer was a big electric switch. I put my hand on the switch, and smiled. 'Goodbye, Al,' I said. Then I switched the electricity off.

The blue lights went off, and the quiet noise stopped. It was very dark. But I didn't go. For a long time I just stood there. I wanted to be sure.

After about twenty minutes, the sound began. Noises, from inside the freezer. I switched on my flashlight and looked at it.

The freezer was full of gas, like a cloud. The gas came from the ice; it made small noises. I waited another ten minutes, until I was sure. There was more gas, more small noises. The freezer was getting warmer!

Very quietly I went upstairs, and out of the front door. I smiled. 'Al,' I thought, 'you are really dying now! And when you are dead, all this is going to belong to me! And the Futures can drive away in their stupid car!'

Happily, I touched the big black car with my hand. And that was my big mistake. Because . . .

BEEP! BEEP! BEEP! The car had an alarm, and it made

The freezer was full of gas, like a cloud.

a very loud noise. It also turned the car's lights on – on, off, on, off, on, off . . .

Quickly, I began to run to my car, two hundred yards away. But a police car came round the corner and saw me! Two policemen got out, took hold of my arms, and pushed me into their car.

'OK, what's all this?' one man said. 'Black clothes, three in the morning, car alarm – I think we've got a car thief, Pete!'

'Yeah!' The other man touched my face with his hand. 'A young woman, too! OK, let's take her to the station.'

7

In court

I arrived at the police station at 3.15 a.m., and said nothing. The Futures arrived at 3.45. 'It was our car,' Dan said. 'Someone tried to steal it.'

'Yeah, OK, sir,' a policeman answered. 'We've got the woman here.'

Then I said: 'You stole my house, so I wanted to steal your car. That's OK, isn't it?' It wasn't true, but it gave me time. While we were all talking in the police station, Al was getting warmer every minute.

So we talked angrily from 4 a.m. until 5. I loved it! Then

31

the Futures had to write their story on three pieces of paper for the police, so it was after six o'clock when they went back to the house. And I was happy, because I knew they were too late. *By now,* I thought, *Al won't be frozen. He'll just be dead.*

Of course, they found out. At eight o'clock the Futures came back and there was a lot of trouble. 'Al's dead!' they shouted. 'You killed him! You switched off the freezer and killed your brother!'

I laughed. 'Of course I didn't,' I said. 'He was dead already. I just saved you some electricity!'

❧→➤●◄←❧

That's why I'm here in court today. The police called me a murderer, and all the newspapers wrote about me. And so of course now I have not one, but *two* really good lawyers! The lawyers are free, because I have no money, but I *am* famous, and they want to be on TV. And because of my expensive lawyers, the police and the Futures look really stupid.

'Al Shore was dead,' my lawyers say, again and again. 'He was already dying of AIDS, and then he took a dangerous sleeping drug. Either he took the drug himself, or the Futures gave it to him. And then the Futures put him in a freezer and froze his body to $-196°$ Celsius. Nobody can stay alive when they're just a piece of ice. So

'Al's dead!' they shouted. 'You killed him!'

the Futures are the murderers, not his sister Ellen. When she switched off the freezer, he was already dead. How can anybody kill a dead man?'

Every day, people write about this in the newspapers, and talk about it on TV. Most people think I'm right, and the Futures are wrong. Last week, a newspaper tried to give me $100,000 for my story, but my lawyers told me to wait. And this week, another newspaper tried to give me $200,000! This is the last week of the trial. Soon, I'm going to be free.

Free – and rich too! At last!

I tell the court the story of our family.

Today, my lawyers asked me questions in court, and I told my story. Then they sat down, and the police lawyer stood up.

The police lawyer is a young woman with short dark hair. She talks very quickly, in a hard, strong voice. She is clever, I know, but it doesn't matter now. She found only one doctor who thinks that cryonics is possible. We found four very famous doctors who don't. They say that Al was dead *before* I switched the freezer off, either because of

34

the sleeping drug, or because of the cold. So how could I kill a dead man?

'Ms Shore, did you love your brother?' she asks.

I laugh. 'No, not really.'

'Oh? Why not?' There is a small smile on her face.

I tell the court the story of our family. How our parents gave Al everything, and me nothing. How Al gave me nothing – only our parents' old house. How I cleaned his house for him, and cooked at parties. How I helped him when he was sick, but he gave me nothing.

My lawyers look unhappy, but it doesn't matter. Nothing matters now. Next week I'm going to be free!

'Your brother was very sick. He had AIDS. Did you know that?'

'I know now, because Dan Future told me. After Al was dead. I didn't know before.'

'I see. But you knew that your brother was sick, and you bought medicine for him, didn't you?'

'Yes, I did.'

'Why didn't he go to a doctor?'

'Because I'm a nurse, and his sister. He trusted me.'

'That's right. He trusted you, his sister.' The lawyer looks at me. For a long minute she is silent. I begin to feel cold and afraid. She takes a police bag from under her table, opens it, and slowly takes out a syringe. She holds it up, in front of my face.

'Look at this, Ms Shore. Have you seen it before?'

'I don't know. Maybe.'

'Maybe, you say. But it has your fingerprints on it, Ms Shore. It came from the hospital, and we found it by your brother's bed, with two other syringes. You stole them from the hospital and gave them to your brother, didn't you?'

There is a long silence. In a very small voice, I say: 'All right, maybe I did.'

'Why did you steal them?'

'Look at this, Ms Shore. Have you seen it before?'

'Why? To help Al, of course. To help him to play good music. He wanted clean drugs.' I tell her what Al said to me.

'Clean drugs, you say? Do you know what was in this syringe, Ms Shore?'

'Clean safe drugs.'

'Oh no, Ms Shore. These drugs weren't clean or safe. These syringes also had bacteria in them – very dangerous bacteria. Bacteria that can kill a strong, healthy person. Bacteria that will kill a person with AIDS very quickly. And perhaps a while ago – who knows? – there was another syringe, a dirty syringe, not from a hospital but from a drug user in the streets. A syringe that gave your brother AIDS.'

The police lawyer puts the syringe down on the table, and looks at me again.

'But we found these three syringes by your brother's bed, with your fingerprints on them. Do you know why they had these dangerous bacteria in them?'

'No . . . of course not.'

'Don't you, Ms Shore? Well, that's strange, because I know why they were there. And I think everyone in this courtroom knows why they were there, too. You hated your brother, didn't you? Because he was rich and you were poor, and he gave you nothing. And you stole drugs and syringes for him, because he *trusted* you! He trusted you, his sister, the nurse!'

She looks at the people in the court, a small smile on her young face. 'But that was your brother's big mistake, wasn't it, Ms Shore? You wanted him to die, because you wanted his money and his big house – just like the Futures! So you gave him syringes with dangerous bacteria in them, because you wanted to kill him!'

The court is very quiet now, and everyone is looking at me. But there is nothing I can say. Nothing. Because it is all true.

'You didn't kill your brother when you switched off the

The court is very quiet now, and everyone is looking at me.

freezer, Ms Shore. We all know that now. But you *were* trying to kill him. Slowly, week by week, month by month, you were trying to murder him. Dirty syringes, dirty drugs, dangerous bacteria – you wanted to give him a slow, terrible death. I think that this court will want to send you to prison for a very long time, Ellen Shore!'

I look around the courtroom at the faces. Hundreds of eyes are looking at me, and they all hate me, all of them. No one understands me, no one loves me, no one wants to save me.

No one.

I feel nothing, at first. Then I begin to feel cold, like ice. Like a body in a freezer.

GLOSSARY

AIDS   a very serious and dangerous illness

alarm *(n)*   a loud sound which tells people that something wrong or dangerous is happening

apartment   a flat; a group of rooms in a building where you can live

bacteria   the smallest forms of life which are found in all living and dead animals and plants; some bacteria cause illnesses

card   a small piece of hard paper

care *(v)*   to think that something is important or interesting

clean   not dirty

company   people who work together in a business

crazy   we say someone is crazy when they do strange or dangerous things

cure *(v)*   to make a sick person well

doll   a toy that looks like a person

dream *(n)*   pictures in your head when you are asleep

drugs   dangerous things which people eat or inject, and which make them feel happy or excited for a short time

drunk *(adj)*   doing strange or wild things because of drinking a lot of alcohol

electricity   power that can make heat and light

fingerprints   marks that your fingers make when you touch something

flashlight   a small electric light which you hold in your hand

freezer   a machine that makes food (or other things) very cold

freeze (past tense **froze**)   to make something very cold

frozen   very cold, and hard like ice

gas   anything like air, which you usually cannot see

guilty   if you are guilty, you have done something bad or wrong

hate *(v)*   to dislike very strongly; the opposite of 'to love'

healthy   well and strong; not ill

heart attack   a sudden illness when the heart stops working and sometimes the person dies

ice   water which is very cold and hard like rock

idea   when you think of something new

kids   children

law court   a place where judges and lawyers ask questions and decide if someone is a criminal or not

lawyer   someone who helps people with the law

look after   to take care of something; to keep it safe

maybe   perhaps

medicine   something to eat or drink that helps you to get better when you are ill

motorbike   a bicycle with an engine

record *(n)*   a round thing which plays music through a record-player

rock band   a group of people who play pop or rock music

safe   not dangerous

save   to take someone out of danger

science   the study of natural things (physics, biology, etc. are sciences)

shut up   a rude way of saying 'be quiet'

sick   ill

swimming pool   a special place or building for swimming

switch *(v and n)*   to press something (e.g. a switch on a wall) to turn electricity on or off

syringe   an instrument with a needle which is used to inject medicines or drugs through the skin

tennis court a place where people play tennis (a ball game)

tour *(n)* a journey to visit a lot of places

training learning how to do a job

trial when people go to a law court to decide if someone is a criminal

trust *(v)* to feel sure that someone is good, strong, right, etc.

view what you can see from a window, a mountain top, etc.

whisky a strong alcoholic drink, from Scotland

Before Reading

1 Read the story introduction on the first page of the book, and the back cover. How much do you know now about Ellen Shore and her brother Al? Tick one box for each sentence.

	YES	NO
1 They are American.	☐	☐
2 Al is older than Ellen.	☐	☐
3 Their parents like Ellen more than Al.	☐	☐
4 Ellen hates her brother.	☐	☐
5 Al has a big house and a lot of money.	☐	☐
6 Ellen has an easy life.	☐	☐
7 Ellen has three children.	☐	☐
8 Al steals drugs from the hospital.	☐	☐

2 What is going to happen in the story? Can you guess? Tick one box for each sentence.

	YES	NO	PERHAPS
1 Ellen gets a big house like Al's.	☐	☐	☐
2 Al gives Ellen a lot of money.	☐	☐	☐
3 Ellen kills Al.	☐	☐	☐
4 Al's strange friends kill him.	☐	☐	☐
5 Al dies in an accident.	☐	☐	☐
6 Ellen dies before Al.	☐	☐	☐

While Reading

Read Chapters 1 and 2, and answer these questions.

1 Who is telling the story, and where is she now?
2 Why was Ellen unhappy after Al was born?
3 Why did Ellen's dolls always get sick and die?
4 How old was Ellen when she left home?
5 Why was Ellen unhappy with John?
6 How did Al get rich and famous?
7 Why did Al get sick?
8 What did Ellen tell him to do?

Before you read Chapter 3, can you guess what happens next? Tick one box for each sentence.

		YES	NO
1	Ellen and Al have more good times together.	☐	☐
2	Al starts taking drugs again and gets very ill.	☐	☐
3	Ellen asks Al for some money.	☐	☐
4	Ellen makes a secret plan to get Al's money.	☐	☐

Read Chapter 3, and answer these questions.

1 What did Al ask Ellen to do?
2 Why do you think Ellen agreed to do it?

Read Chapters 4 and 5, and then match these halves of sentences.

1 When Al came back from his tour, . . .
2 He had some new friends, the Futures, . . .
3 Dan Future wore a dark suit . . .
4 But Ellen didn't understand . . .
5 Two weeks later Ellen went to Al's house . . .
6 She couldn't find Al . . .
7 The Futures took her down to the music room . . .
8 They told her that Al's body was frozen, . . .
9 The Futures would look after Al's house and money . . .
10 And when there was a cure for AIDS, . . .
11 Ellen was very angry about this . . .

12 and looked like a businessman.
13 but she found the Futures in the garden.
14 while he was sleeping in the freezer.
15 and at first Ellen thought they were boring.
16 but he was not dead.
17 he looked thin and white and sick.
18 because now she could not get Al's house and money.
19 why a businessman wanted to talk about death.
20 and showed her Al's body in the freezer.
21 because she wanted to say Happy Birthday to Al.
22 the doctors would wake Al up and cure him.

Read Chapter 6. Are these sentences true (T) or false (F)? Rewrite the false sentences with the correct information.

1 Ellen paid for an hour of a lawyer's time.

2 The lawyer wasn't sure that he could win.

3 Ellen didn't have a key to Al's house.

4 She cried when she switched the freezer off.

5 She waited because she wanted to be sure that the freezer was getting warmer.

6 When she touched the Futures' car, the alarm went off.

7 The two policemen thought that Ellen was a murderer.

Before you read Chapter 7, can you guess what is going to happen? Choose some of these answers.

1 The Futures switch the electricity on again and Al stays frozen.

2 Al wakes up alive, but dies of AIDS a short time later.

3 Al doesn't wake up and has been dead all the time.

4 Ellen goes to prison for trying to kill Al.

5 The Futures also go to prison for trying to kill Al.

6 Ellen gets Al's house and money.

7 The Futures get Al's house and money.

Now read Chapter 7 and answer this question.

Who *really* killed Al Shore – Ellen or the Futures? Or were they all guilty? What do *you* think?

After Reading

1 **Complete this passage with these linking words.**

and / at first / because / but / then / when / while

Ellen was angry with the Futures _____ they were going to
look after Al's money. _____ Ellen did not know what to
do, but _____ she had an idea. She went to Al's house
_____ switched the freezer off. She left the house quietly,
_____ the police caught her _____ they heard the car
alarm. They took her to the police station and _____ they
were all talking, Al's body was getting warmer and warmer.

2 **Why did Ellen want to kill her brother? How many of these
answers do *you* think are good ones?**

Ellen wanted to kill Al because . . .

1 she was crazy.
2 Al was very unkind to her.
3 her parents didn't love her and always put Al first.
4 she wanted Al's money for herself.
5 she wanted Al's money for her children.
6 Al was rich and famous and she wasn't.
7 she had an unhappy life with John.
8 she was the kind of person who hated everybody.

3 **Here is a conversation between Al and Dan Future, but it is in the wrong order. Write it out in the correct order and put in the speakers' names. Dan speaks first (number 5).**

1 _____ 'But . . . does freezing make these people healthy again?'

2 _____ 'Well, yes, I think maybe I do. Tell me, Mr Future, how much does this freezing cost . . .?'

3 _____ 'Well, it's the science of freezing people.'

4 _____ 'But why do you keep these people alive? They'll still be ill when they wake up, won't they?'

5 _____ 'Hi, I'm Dan Future. I work with cryonics.'

6 _____ 'Freezing people? Why do you do that?'

7 _____ 'Cryonics? What's that?'

8 _____ 'You mean, medicines to cure illnesses which kill people today?'

9 _____ 'No, it can't make them healthy. It just keeps their bodies alive for hundreds of years.'

10 _____ 'We freeze people to save their lives, Al. People who are very ill, and who are going to die because doctors can't help them.'

11 _____ 'That's right, Al. For example, doctors can't cure AIDS today, but in a hundred years' time maybe they can. Do you know anybody with AIDS?'

12 _____ 'Yes, they'll still be ill in a hundred years' time. But there'll be new medicines by then, you see – better medicines!'

4 **Here are two different newspaper stories about Ellen and Al. Use the words to fill in the gaps in each story.**

STORY 1

criminals, dead, drug, electricity, froze, killed, prison, sick, steal, switched, true, trusted

Ellen Shore didn't kill her brother Al. She _____ off the _____ to the freezer, that's _____, but Al was already _____ when she did that. The people who _____ Al Shore were the Futures. They gave a dangerous sleeping _____ to a _____ man, and _____ his body to −196°C. That's what killed him. Poor Al Shore _____ the Futures, but they are _____ who wanted to _____ a rich man's money. They must go to _____, and Ellen must be free!

STORY 2

bacteria, cure, die, dying, fingerprints, freezer, guilty, healthy, medicine, murderer, save

Ellen Shore is _____ of murder. First she tried to kill her brother with dangerous _____ in syringes – and her _____ were on those syringes. Poor Al Shore knew he was _____ and he left a letter for us. 'In a hundred years' time,' he wrote, 'there will be a _____ that can _____ AIDS. Then I can wake up and live a long, _____ life.' The Futures wanted to _____ Al's life, not to kill him. But Ellen wanted Al to _____, so she turned off the _____. She is a _____!

50

5 Now match these headlines with Story 1 or Story 2 in the last activity. Which headlines can go with both stories?

ROCK STAR DIES IN FREEZER   NO FUTURE FOR AL

WHO KILLED AL SHORE?   CRAZY CRYONICS!

ELLEN SHORE — GUILTY!   SISTER MURDERS BROTHER

BE CAREFUL — THE FUTURES   HOW TO STEAL A RICH MAN'S
   ARE COMING!   HOUSE

6 The story doesn't tell us what happens to Al's house and his money. What do you think the lawyers said? Complete these sentences.

1 The Futures' lawyer: 'The Futures must get Al's house and his money, because _____.'

2 Ellen's lawyer: 'Ellen Shore must get Al's house and his money, because _____.'

7 Is cryonics a good idea or not? Do you agree (A) or disagree (D) with these sentences? Explain why.

1 Only rich people can pay for cryonics.

2 People like the Futures are criminals.

3 Cryonics will make a lot of people happy.

4 We must only freeze important people.

5 We must only freeze very ill people.

6 Cryonics is everybody's future.

ABOUT THE AUTHOR

Tim Vicary is an experienced teacher and writer, and has written several stories for the Oxford Bookworms Library. Many of these are in the Thriller & Adventure series, such as *White Death* (at Stage 1) or in the True Stories series, such as *Grace Darling* (at Stage 2), which tells the story of a girl who became a famous heroine when she helped to rescue people from a shipwreck. He has also published two long novels, *The Blood upon the Rose* and *Cat and Mouse*.

Tim Vicary has two children, and keeps dogs, cats, and horses. He lives and works in York, in the north of England.

ABOUT BOOKWORMS

OXFORD BOOKWORMS LIBRARY

Classics • True Stories • Fantasy & Horror • Human Interest
Crime & Mystery • Thriller & Adventure

The OXFORD BOOKWORMS LIBRARY offers a wide range of original and adapted stories, both classic and modern, which take learners from elementary to advanced level through six carefully graded language stages:

Stage 1 (400 headwords)	**Stage 4** (1400 headwords)
Stage 2 (700 headwords)	**Stage 5** (1800 headwords)
Stage 3 (1000 headwords)	**Stage 6** (2500 headwords)

More than fifty titles are also available on cassette, and there are many titles at Stages 1 to 4 which are specially recommended for younger learners. In addition to the introductions and activities in each Bookworm, resource material includes photocopiable test worksheets and Teacher's Handbooks, which contain advice on running a class library and using cassettes, and the answers for the activities in the books.

Several other series are linked to the OXFORD BOOKWORMS LIBRARY. They range from highly illustrated readers for young learners, to playscripts, non-fiction readers, and unsimplified texts for advanced learners.

Oxford Bookworms Starters	*Oxford Bookworms Factfiles*
Oxford Bookworms Playscripts	*Oxford Bookworms Collection*

Details of these series and a full list of all titles in the OXFORD BOOKWORMS LIBRARY can be found in the *Oxford English* catalogues. A selection of titles from the OXFORD BOOKWORMS LIBRARY can be found on the next pages.

Sherlock Holmes Short Stories

SIR ARTHUR CONAN DOYLE
Retold by Clare West

Sherlock Holmes is the greatest detective of them all. He sits in his room, and smokes his pipe. He listens, and watches, and thinks. He listens to the steps coming up the stairs; he watches the door opening – and he knows what question the stranger will ask.

In these three of his best stories, Holmes has three visitors to the famous flat in Baker Street – visitors who bring their troubles to the only man in the world who can help them.

Ear-rings from Frankfurt

REG WRIGHT

Richard Walton is in trouble again. He has lost his job, and he has borrowed money from his sister, Jennifer – again. And now he has disappeared. Jennifer is looking for him, and so are the police. They both have some questions that they want to ask him.

How did he lose his job? Why did he fly to Frankfurt? Who gave his girlfriend those very expensive gold ear-rings?   -

Only Richard can answer these questions. But nobody can find Richard.

Dead Man's Island

JOHN ESCOTT

Mr Ross lives on an island where no visitors come. He stops people from taking photographs of him. He is young and rich, but he looks sad. And there is one room in his house which is always locked.

Carol Sanders and her mother come to the island to work for Mr Ross. Carol soon decides that there is something very strange about Mr Ross. Where did he get his money from? How can a young man buy an island? So she watches, and she listens – and one night she learns what is behind the locked door.

The Death of Karen Silkwood

JOYCE HANNAM

This is the story of Karen Silkwood. It begins with her death.

Why does her story begin where it should end? Certain people wanted her death to be an ending. Why? What were they afraid of? Karen Silkwood had something to tell us, and she believed that it was important. Why didn't she live to tell us? Will we ever know what really happened? The questions go on and on, but there are no answers.

This is a true story. It happened in Oklahoma, USA, where Karen Silkwood lived and worked . . . and died.

The Mystery of Allegra
PETER FOREMAN

Allegra is an unusual name. It means 'happy' in Italian, but the little girl in this story is sometimes very sad. She is only five years old, but she tells Adrian, her new friend, that she is going to die soon. How does she know?

And who is the other Allegra? The girl in a long white nightdress, who has golden hair and big blue eyes. The girl who comes only at night, and whose hands and face are cold, so cold . . .

As the Inspector Said and Other Stories
RETOLD BY JOHN ESCOTT

The murder plan seems so neat, so clever. How can it possibly fail? And when Sonia's stupid, boring little husband is dead, she will be free to marry her handsome lover. But perhaps the boring little husband is not so stupid after all . . .

Murder plans that go wrong, a burglar who makes a bad mistake, a famous jewel thief who meets a very unusual detective . . . These five stories from the golden age of crime writing are full of mystery and surprises.